Spare the Rod and Spoil the Child

Rev. Dr. James Cotton, PhD

ISBN –9798666757956

This book is printed in the United States of America

To order additional copies of this book, contact:
www.amazon.com

Dedication

To my loving wife, Deaconess Margaret Cotton who has been my supportive anchor for 73 years and a church usher for 88 years.
To my friend, Veronica Everette, for extending a listening ear and support throughout this book production process.

Agape Love

Like all parents, we love our children with Agape love, that is the love of Jesus Christ. In a Godly family, we try to express our love so we will have a lasting bond with our children, hoping they will receive our values as they grow up and have that love and respect as long as we live.

"Train up a child in the way he should go, and when he is old, he will not depart from it." Proverbs 22:6

Table of Contents

Preface

Looking back on my life ...

I was born and raised on a small farm in rural North Carolina, along with four siblings: I, the youngest. My parents were hardworking Christians, who were dedicated to the teachings of the church and always sort to follow scripture in the upbringing of me and my sister and brothers. We were expected to carry out required chores on the farm six days a week. Sundays were devoted to the church. *Leviticus 23: 3 states, "Six days shall work be done; but the seventh day is the Sabbath of rest, a holy convocation; ye shall do no work therein; it is the Sabbath of the Lord in all our dwellings".*

My parents did not faulter from God's word and made it a point that we attended church services on a regular basis. We traveled by wagon drawn by a mule to church. I was baptized in a creek near the church. A humble upbringing.

I realized that if I wanted non- essential items,

such as toys, I had to earn my own money. Ultimately, I suppose I became an entrepreneur at a very young age. At 5 years old, I started my first money earning job: picking up trash left by workers who were building a house. I earned fifty cents a week. When I was in the seventh grade, I sold garden and flower seeds. Other jobs followed allowing me to buy my first bicycle when I was thirteen. When I was sixteen, I got my driver's license and purchased my first car. Although I had a car, to save money I walked one mile to the school bus stop when I started high school, which was seven miles away from home.

I grew up when schools were segregated, and for a period, Black children did not have school buses to attend school. So, when I started school, I had to walk 3 ½ miles each day. I did this until I was in the seventh grade. Quite often, I did not have money to buy lunch at school; consequently, I was forced to carry a meager lunch consisting of fatback meat and cornbread.

Maintaining discipline was essential in our household. At a very young age, my siblings and I had specific chores that we had to do each day. Regardless of school or other circumstances, we were expected to complete them and to do them without question.

We were all introduced to the switch if work expectations were not met. My parents strongly believed in and exercised *Proverbs 22:6 which states, "Train up a child in the way he should go, and when he is old, he will not depart from it.*

When we were disobedient or didn't do what our parents perceived as the right thing to do, we were disciplined. Most times my father would whip us with a switch or belt as punishment. But, if he did not explain why we were being punished, our mother with her profound wisdom would always step in to let us know the "why" behind the punishment. She was teaching and guiding us so that we would not make the same mistake in the future, but was instilling in us a sense of dedication, responsibility, and obedience.

Using the switch or belt along with verbal explanation of why we were getting a whipping was my parents' way of teaching these attributes, along with others such as loyalty, integrity, respect, honesty, humbleness, caring, and love in every aspect of our lives. Discipline meant that our parents loved us and wanted the best for us. They were relying on God's word.

As what often take place in the strictest of families, children will continue to be defiant at times. Such was the case with me. It was always my desire to become a doctor. In order for me to do that, it meant my first finishing high school. Finishing school required me to attend five days a week without missing too many days. However, my father's thought processes were a bit different from mine. He thought that one of my responsibilities was to earn extra money for the family. To accomplish this, I had to work on our white neighbor's farm. Doing so would mean my missing two or three days of school each week.

I thought this to be an injustice to me; so, I thought of a way to accomplish both tasks: attending school 5 days a week and working on the white neighbor's farm. Unbeknownst to my parents, I got up around 4 o'clock in the morning, hid my school clothes in the woods, completed my chores at the neighbor's farm, then snuck off to school.

I knew that I was being disobedient, and this behavior would lead to a whipping should my father find out. But, I continued this behavior until I found work driving the school bus. My education meant so much to me.

Unfortunately, I was unable to graduate from school. At the age of eighteen, I was drafted into the United States Army, where I was trained to be a medical tech to assist doctors in the operating room. I enjoyed this assignment because it was right inline with my career goals. Getting my high school diploma was essential if I were to be a doctor so after my discharge from the army, I returned to high school to complete the twelfth grade. I did so with honors.

In later years, my wife and I used God's teachings and the disciplinary actions used by our parents to raise our children. In doing so, our children have grown into successful, law abiding citizens and followers of God's words.

We all want the best for our children. We must show them the way. We must discipline them.

Introduction
Our Children Are Our Future

Spare the rod, spoil the child is a familiar adage, believed by many. I tend to put much value in the adage because as a Christian and a follower of the Word (the Bible), it does coincide with scriptures found throughout the Bible, but most notably in Proverbs. To name a few: *"The rod and reproof give wisdom; but a child left to himself bringeth his mother to shame." Proverbs 29:15*
"Withhold not correction from the child; for it thou beatest him with the rod, he shall not die. Proverbs 23:13 "He that spareth his rod hateth his son, but he that loveth him chasteneth him betimes." Proverbs 13:24
"Thou shall beat him with the rod, and shalt deliver his soul from hell.' Proverbs 23:14

Teaching and guiding our children is an essential responsibility of any parent. We all want our children to be productive members of society, but sometimes we fail because we do not carry out our responsibility. We should never forget that we as parents set the course of our children's fate, their future. So, through God's teachings, his direction, we can fulfill our parenting responsibilities and set the course for our children achieving high expectations and living a productive life.

In this book, I will use scripture, personal experiences, observations, and articles of research to show how "spare the rod and spoil the child" does have truth and should be taken seriously.

We will examine the meaning of the word "rod" and determine how God intended its use. Suggested potential positive outcomes of using the rod and conversely the negative outcomes of not using the rod will also be reviewed.

It is my belief that spiritually aligned discipline is the key to raising children to not only become productive members of the society, but also ones who will not fall to the ills of some of societal negative influences. Influences such as violence on tv, in video games, and even peer pressure. Once guidance is set and consequences are set and followed in the household, it will reach beyond to include choices made outside of the parent's watchful eye.

Note that we will be discussing "spiritually aligned" discipline and that scriptures will be used to solidify each area discussed. I want to distinguish between the type of discipline that God has ordained versus negative punishment that is not in line with what God seeks.

For those critics who do not believe in physical punishment, we will discuss the difference and relay how parents can use a 2-prong disciplinary approach as a healthy way to guide children on the right path.

Part 1
Spare the Rod, Spoil the Child: A Close Look At Its Meaning

Dictionary Meaning

1. Rod - A stick or bundle of twigs used to punish.
2. Rod -To impose a penalty on for a fault, offense, or violation.
3. Rod - To inflict injury or hurt.
4. Rod- A parent must discipline their children, implies punishing aimed at reforming an offender.

"Spare the rod, spoil the child." Controversial—to say the least. But the phrase is closely akin to Proverbs13:24. The King James translation states *"He that spareth his rod hateth his son: But he who loves him chasteneth him betimes."* Scripturally, the intent is guiding/ disciplining our children so that they will know right from wrong.

Controversy comes into play because of the interpretation of that simple word "rod". Many just look at the dictionary meaning: a stick or pole. Those who do so tend to substitute the stick or pole with a belt, switch, or a paddle when it comes to disciplining a child. But, disciplining means more than punishing a child. Its primary meaning is to teach and/or guide. The afore mentioned rods only punish; they do not teach or guide.

However, from my viewpoint, "rod" can also refer to verbally letting the child know what he has done wrong, to indicate what should be done, or to show him. This is guiding and/or teaching children. *Deuteronomy 6:7 says "And thou shall teach diligently unto thy children, and shall talk of them when thou sittest in thine house, and when thou walkest by the way, and when thou liest down, and when thou risest up." Proverbs 1:5 further asserts, "A wise man may hear, will increase learning And a man of understanding shall attain undo wise counsel."*

In other words, disciplining is the practice of teaching your child what type of behavior is acceptable and what type is not acceptable. Discipline brings stability and structure into a child's life.

Growing up on a farm, as I previously mentioned, my parents gave me daily chores to complete. If for no good reason, I did not complete those chores, my parents had no problem putting a switch to my legs. Believe me, there were very few times when those chores were not done and done correctly. I did not want to feel the sting of that switch.

Most times, my father used the switch (sometimes the belt) to discipline us. However, it was my mother, her wisdom that brought balance to the disciplinary process. That is, she offset my father's act of punishment with teaching and guidance.

Quite often she would tell me, "Son, your daddy loves you. The reason he punished you is that he wants you to know right from wrong. He wants to teach you things that are important and will help you in life." My mother would go on to say, "Son, if you attend church and learn about the love of Jesus Christ and His goodness, that goodness will help keep you from many pitfalls in life. That will also keep you out of trouble. He wants you to grow up to be a trustworthy man, a man that can stand out in the community and help others. One day, you will thank your father. *Proverbs 22:6 says train up a child in the way he should go, and when he is old, he will never depart from it."* This is one of the most important verses in Proverbs." She went on to say, "When a child is raised in a Godly home and raised in a church setting, the Holy Spirit is with him always to remind him or her of the pitfalls of life. If a situation arises, and is not of Jesus Christ, the Holy Spirit will step in."

A child who is not disciplined will not know right from wrong. Discipline is a show of love.

Proverbs 23:13 - "Do not withhold discipline from a child; if you punish him with the rod, he will not die."

Points To Remember

In the time scripture was written, and even today, parents use various tools to guide their children. The use of the switch (or belt) is not the only means of discipling children. The objective of discipline is to influence positive behavior in children. This is done through teaching/guiding, showing the child how he/she is to respond in given situations. These acts of discipline allow children to develop self-discipline, and help them become emotionally and socially mature, secure adults. Children becoming self-disciplined is directly related to the teachings of *Proverbs 22:6, which says, "Train up a child in the way he should go, and when he is old he will not depart from it."*

The switch (rod) along with love(rod) was the type of disciplinary action that helped me to acquire many attributes I found essential in later life. Had I not been disciplined through love and God's teachings; I might not have learned some very valuable qualities

Part 2
More on Discipline and Its Importance

Why is discipline necessary when raising a child? Fair question; simple answer.

Discipline is essential for children to develop into health, happy individuals. It serves as the cornerstone for them to develop many attributes that they will need as they mature into adult hood. In other words, discipline is all about training children; not punishing them. Training; that is, guiding and teaching are the components of discipline. When we guide and teach consistently then we are more apt to achieve the long-term goals and objectives we set for our children.

I think we can all agree that some aspect of discipline is essential and that's an easy answer. But, a more difficult question to answer perhaps is "what is the best way to discipline". Different situations may call for different techniques or a combination of techniques. Let's take a look at a few scenarios to see what particular technique will yield the long-term objectives that we want to achieve.

So keep in mind as we review these scenarios that effective discipline uses many different tools (methods, techniques). As parents we must be very mindful of the tool we use in our efforts for our children to learn positive behavior to replace negative behavior. Therefore, when you're considering a discipline method, ask yourself if that method will guide and instruct your child to be more like the adjectives you chose.

Let me reiterate: ask yourself, how would you approach these situations? What disciplinary technique (s) would you use?

Scenario 1

By nature, children are inquisitive; there is a continuous thirst to learn, to explore. Think about the 2- year olds – the terrible two's – as we sometimes refer. These little ones are into everything. Toddler Andy is crawling around on the kitchen floor and spots pieces of food on the floor. He immediately crawls over, picks up some, and puts it in his mouth. As a parent, you do not want him to eat discarded food from the floor.

What do you do to help this child begin to become self-disciplined so that he will not repeat? Do you, do nothing? Do you, say a strong "NO, you could get hurt?" Do you, say "no, you may get hurt" and give a little tap on the hands? Do you just give a tap on the hands?

Scenario 2

Johnnie is a second grader who bullies George, a classmate. He calls George names and teases him because he is overweight. Johnnie's teacher has observed his behavior, has spoken to him about his behavior. But Johnnie continues to bully. The teacher has decided to inform his mother about his behavior.

What should Johnnie's mother do to teach him compassion and caring about others? Should she pull out the belt? Should she yell at him? Should she just ignore the teacher and hope for the best? Or should she do something else?

Scenario 3

Fourteen year- old Karen and her ten year-old brother Jason are forever feuding about something. One evening the two were watching TV. Karen wanted to watch The Price Is Right, her favorite game show, while Jason wanted to watch a rerun of the Dukes of Hazard. They both were switching the TV channels back and forth. Karen suddenly hit Jason in the face causing his nose to bleed. Margie, their mother, suddenly appeared in the room and learned that Karen had punched Jason. She sent Karen to her room and grounded (no TV) her for a week.

Do you think that grounding Karen will improve Karen and Jason's relationship? How would you have handled the situation?

Scenario 4

Miss Harris, Shirley's neighbor, asked her to baby sit one evening. Shirley had been doing so for the past 6 months without incident. Standard rule: no friends allowed.

Soon after Miss Harris left the house, Shirley received a call from her boyfriend, Patrick, who wanted to come over and watch TV with her. Shirley explained that she could not have anyone over while she baby sat. Patrick, however persuaded Shirley to let him come over; he would leave before Miss Harris returned.

Unfortunately for Patrick and Shirley, Miss

Harris returned home early and found Patrick there. Miss Harris told Patrick he had to leave; told Karen she would not be asking her to baby sit again; called Karen's mother and told her what had happened.

What disciplinary measures (if any) should Karen's mother take to teach her to be responsible, reliable, and follow rules?

Teaching your child to know right from wrong; how to respond in certain situations is no easy task. We as parents are constantly learning ourselves what works and what does not work. Does merely punishing the child get long-lasting positive results or does it cause the child to rebel continuing to exhibit inappropriate behavior?

As I mentioned earlier, growing up, my father most times used either the switch or belt to discipline. So, I generally thought of my parents as strict disciplinarians. If any one of their five children were disobedient, misbehaved, disrespectful, or dishonest, they had no problem using the belt or switch on us. Although these rods were used, they were always used in combination with an explanation of why we were being disciplined.

In my opinion, the key to effective discipline is using corrective measures that will result in positive changed behavior. A show of love is vital. Don't just use the switch (rod), but also use explanation (rod) and a show of love (rod) in combination for a more effective disciplinary tool that is grounded by the bible. Keep in mind, the physical punishment and the explanation don't have to be from the same parent: my father took on the physical disciplinarian role, while my mother took on the explanation role. However, it is important that both show love.

During my youth, school officials and teachers could also discipline children. Often referred to as corporal punishment, they used a belt or paddle to discipline when a child was disobedient or misbehaved. This process was used with the understanding that the teachers would use "reasonable" force and not cause injury. Though not widely used today, there are some states that still use this type of corrective measure.

I view corporal punishment as "punishment". It does not teach or guide. Children, however, may change their behavior out of fear of getting paddled. Furthermore, corporal punishment can be embarrassing and humiliating. I can strongly attest to this.

When I was in the third grade, I got the paddle because I misspelled three words on a spelling test. That was the one and only time that I was paddled in school. I made sure that I got 100% on my spelling tests after that first encounter with the paddle. In fact, I became the best spelling in my class. For me, the fear of being paddled made me spend sufficient time to learn my spelling words.

Although in this instance there were positive results, however, this is not always the case. "A mother of a student with autism reported that her son's behavior changed after he was struck in his Florida school: "He's an avoider by nature, before he was never aggressive. Now, he struggles with anger; right after the incidents he'd have anger explosions." (Joint HRW/ACLU Committee, 2010)

According to the Center for Effective Discipline, "critics argue paddling does not stop bad behavior, while supporters say paddling teaches discipline and respect."

Derrick Johnson, President and CEO, National Association for the Advancement of Colored

People (NAACP), presented a report that shows, “within schools where it(corporal punishment) is practiced, the impact falls disproportionately on black children and children with disabilities.”

Quite unfortunate. That’s why I am not in favor of corporal punishment being administered in schools. Discriminatory practice is often evident

******

We are all familiar with the statement “it takes a village to raise a child”. This belief was strongly evident during my youth. A neighbor could get involved in helping to raise another person’s children. In many instances, they also had “understood permission” to discipline (verbally) a neighbor’s child. And sometimes other family members or close acquaintances had permission to use the switch.

Time and time again, I watched as my neighbors stepped into the disciplinary process. This had a dramatic positive effect on us and other local children. I can honestly say that there was a show of respect, a change in behavior in many of my friends and associates.

Times have changed though. Many of today’s parents do not even want a neighbor to chastise or correct their child in any fashion. If an attempt is made to correct a child, it's not surprising to hear a parent say, "Raise your own children and leave mine alone". This could be a bad decision because if a child is out of the view of his parent, he might think that he can do whatever he wants and get away with what could be considered bad behavior. Exercised over time, this could result in affecting the child's development negatively.

******

Time out, grounding, taking away a cell phone or some favorite item, threating to tell "your father" are among a growing list of techniques that we take in our efforts to discipline our children. Some work, some do not.

As I mentioned before, raising our children is no easy task. It is the parents' duty; their responsibility to teach them. Without discipline, the child is left to figure things out for himself; make his own decisions. Sometimes those decisions may be the wrong decisions. A parent must step in. I believe if we lean more on the teachings of our Heavenly Father, we will achieve our parental goals.

Deuteronomy 6:2 "That thou mightiest fear the Lord thy God. To keep all his statutes and His commandments, which I command thee, thou and thy son, and thy son's son, all the days of thy life; and that thy days may be prolonged."

Part 3
Possible Effects of Discipling

I must first point out and make perfectly clear that in my opinion, the primary characteristics of discipline are guiding and teaching; NOT punishment. Discipline is essential and must be exercised; for It sets limits, shows direction, provides knowledge, displays love.

Our children enter this world totally dependent upon being taught and guided in every aspect of their lives. They do not know right from wrong; they must be taught. Since this is the case, then that aspect of their growth and development, has to start at a very early age and must be consistent.

Exercising discipline is a show of love and can be directly related to children developing some very essential characteristics; such as, integrity, honesty, obedience, respect, humbleness, caring/kindness—among others.

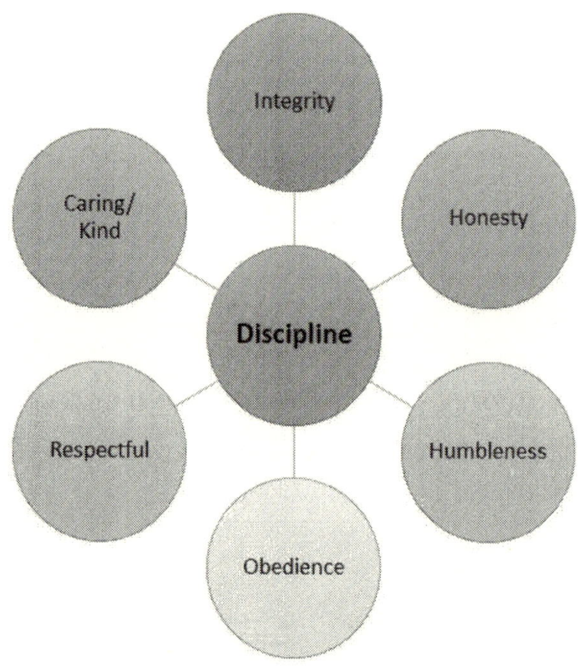

Let's take a few minutes to take a look at these characteristics and see how they can become an integral part of our children's personality.

Integrity

Webster defines integrity as the practice of being honest and sharing a consistent and uncompromising adherence to strong moral and ethical principles and values. In ethics, integrity is regarded as the honesty and truthfulness or accuracy of one's actions.

The heart of integrity is always to do what is right. *Proverbs 20:7 says, "The righteous who walks in his integrity— his children are blessed after him."*

Just how do we achieve this? That is, "to always do what is right". It should not be too difficult, if we follow God's Word.

We are familiar with the Ten Commandments. These Commandments are in place in order to help us build integrity through following guidelines that mold our character. When we teach our children the commandments and encourage them to follow them, it allows them to learn right from wrong and gives them basic principles that help them build integrity.

Let's take a look at these scriptures and see how by following them, integrity can be exemplified in our character. If we, as parents, follow these commandments ourselves, then we can teach our children to strive to attain the same.

The Ten Commandments, Exodus 20:1-17 are laws given by God as guidelines for daily living.

The first eleven verses govern our relationship to God, while verses 12–17 speak to our relationship to other people. Let's look at each of these verses (verses 12-17) to see how integrity comes into play.

Verse 12 "Honor thy father and thy mother: that thy days may be long upon the land which the Lord thy God giveth thee." If we honor our parents, then we respect and obey them; tell them the truth and follow their teachings. Children will try us and see just how far they can go. Whenever we discover that children are being disrespectful or disobeying, we have to correct the situation right then and there. If children get away with something once; expect them to try again.

By correcting our children at home, it helps them understand the importance of obeying and respecting people in authority outside the home.

Verse 13 "Thou shall not kill." We do not take it upon ourselves to end someone else's life; regardless of the circumstance or situation. Children are exposed to crime in so many avenues these days: from television programs to videos to electronic games to street gangs.

Too many times, in this day and age, children become numb to death and violence. Playing video games that depict characters being killed over and over again, only to get up and do it all over again as if nothing was wrong, puts a false reality in some kids and they often don't understand the finality of someone dying. Often, kids will shoot, stab, or use other objects on someone, only to believe that once they fall, like the video game, they will get up again and things will be okay.

Consequently, parents must always be aware of the interests and interactions of their children. They must reference God's teachings and the value of life.

It is a sin to not only take another's life, but also think of or wish harm to someone else. Following this commandment means that we respect and value the lives of others.

Verse 14 "Thou shall not comment adultery." Being true to your spouse. This means practicing ethical and moral behavior and respecting the institution of marriage. How is this concept conveyed to a child?

Remember children watch their parents' actions and they listen to what their parents say. They will emulate their parents. If they observe a parent cheating, then they might get the idea that it is ok to be unfaithful. Conversely, when they observe parents showing affection for one another; being respectful of each other's wishes, then children will learn that marriage is special. That it is not ok to be unfaithful, but to cherish and respect their partner.

Verse 15 "Thou shall not steal." Do not take something that belongs to someone else. Ethical behavior again comes into play; in addition to being respectful of other people's property.

Parents can start when children are at a very young age to teach this concept. When a toddler picks up a toy from day care, claims it as his own and subsequently brings it home, it's the parent's responsibility to let the child know that he cannot bring home the toy not belonging to him. And then, must have the child take the toy back.

We all know that such instances may occur time and time again. Well, parents must correct each time until the child learns. We can not afford not to.

Verse 17, "Thou shall not covet thy neighbour's house, thou shalt not covet thy neighbour's wife, nor his manservant, nor his maidservant, nor his ox, nor his ass, nor anything that is thy neighbour's." In essence, be thankful and satisfied with what God has given you; not be envious of others.

I view integrity as a major characteristic that we want our children to possess. Integrity is the foundation of trustworthiness and honesty. Each day means new challenges, new decisions to be made, new problems to be solved.

When faced with such circumstances, we must do and say that which is right at all times, regardless of our surroundings. Integrity is that internal compass that directs us to the direction we should take.

Integrity is not an automatic trait. It is something that can become that special trait through positive discipline – teaching and guiding. A show of integrity is evident when the child does the right thing when no one is watching. *2Corinthians 8:21 'For we are taking pains to do what is right, not only in the eyes of the Lord but also in the eyes of man."*

Other Integrity Related Scripture

Proverbs 10:9 - *He that walketh uprightly walketh surely: but he that perverteth his ways shall be known.*

Proverbs 28:6 - *Better [is] the poor that walketh in his uprightness, than [he that is] perverse [in his] ways, though he [be] rich.*

Proverbs 11:3 - *The integrity of the upright shall guide them: but the perverseness of transgressors shall destroy*

Honesty

I'm sure many of you are familiar with the story about George Washington and the cherry tree.

When I was growing up, as part of my history lessons in school, we were told the story of George Washington and the cherry tree. Well for those of you who have not heard the story, it goes a bit like this.

When George Washington was about 6 years old, his father gave him a hatchet as a gift. One day when he was outside and excited about using his hatchet, young George mistakenly cut down his father's cherry tree. Later, when his father confronted him, George admitted to cutting down the cherry tree—saying to his father, "I cannot tell a lie".

True or not, the story brings out an important characteristic that we should all have and a characteristic that we should instill in our children:HONESTY. *Proverbs 26:28says, "A lying tongue hateth those that are affected by it. And a flattering mouth worketh ruin." Likewise, John 14:6 asserts, "I am the way, the truth and the life. No man cometh unto the father, but by me."*

Our Lord is asking us to be honest with one another; to be free from deceit or being untruthful to ourselves, our children, and others. Honesty plays an important role in our interactions with others. As we interact with others, we too experience that we'd rather be around those who are truthful/honest than those who have a tendency to lie or be untruthful. *Matthew 7:16 tells us that we are known by our fruit."*

Teaching our children to be honest can be a challenging task. And because of this, we must correct our children every time we discover that they have not been truthful about something. This means correcting even when they are toddlers.

How many times have you asked your 2 or 3-year old did they eat the cookie or chocolate candy? They responded "no', but there were cookie crumbs or chocolate covering their face. A "little white lie", perhaps, but a lie still; one that has to be corrected. If not corrected, then that little lie could very well lead into another lie and over time to an even bigger lie.

We all have lied and not been honest at some time; even some of us who are devoted to our faiths and devoted to the Word of God. As I mentioned earlier, I was brought up in a Christian household. We attended church regularly and attended Bible study. We knew right from wrong. We knew the truth from a lie.

However, my parents as well as all of our neighbors and church members all told the infamous "lie" at Christmas: Santa, the fat man in the red suit, would come down the chimney and bring toys and Christmas bags for the children.

I, too, must confess that my wife and I told our children that it was Santa who brought them that bike or that doll or the new clothes when they got up Christmas morning. It was tradition and we did not want to disappoint the children by telling them something different.

Why do we do this? Do we think that our children will be disappointed if they knew that that toy came from us or from grandma or grandpa, instead of Santa? Have we ever asked ourselves if that "little white lie" has had any effect on our children's lives?

Does that "little white lie" cause our children to sometime doubt if we are being truthful to them at all times? Something to think about (maybe).
Ephesians 4:25
"Therefore, each of you must put off falsehood and speak truthfully to your neighbor, for we are all members of one body."

As always, we are the role model. Be honest; tell the truth. We do not want our children to hear us telling a lie. If they do, they might get the impression that it's "ok", and they could very well think that it is ok for them to do so as well. Get into the habit of being truthful all the time.

Colossians 3:9 expresses
" Do not lie to each other, since you have taken off your old self with its practices."

Other Honesty Related Scripture

Proverbs 12:22 - *Lying lips [are] abomination to the LORD: but they that deal truly [are] his delight.*

John 8:32 - *And ye shall know the truth, and the truth shall make you free.*

Proverbs 19:1 - *Better [is] the poor that walketh in his integrity, than [he that is] perverse in his lips, and is a fool.*

2 Corinthians 8:21 - *Providing for honest things, not only in the sight of the Lord, but also in the sight of men.*

Obedience

Being obedient is one way in which we can show God our love and our belief and trust in Him. *"Children, obey your parents in the Lord, for this is right." Ephesians 6:1 and 1 Samuel 15:22 reminds us that "to obey is better than sacrifice."*

Teaching children to obey may not be an easy task. But, it's something that we cannot afford to not do. From the time they are toddlers, we can point out times when our children choose not to obey us. Think about the times that we tell them to walk, not run when they go outside. But, as soon as the door is opened...what do they do? Break out into a run. Doesn't matter that they've been prewarned that the ground is slippery and they might fall if they run. Most times, they've forgotten that warning. I suppose, running is more exciting to them than walking.

Now, don't forget that teen aged son or daughter who sneaks out the house to attend a party or meet with their friends when you've' told them that they can't go out, but they go out anyway. These acts of disobedience must be corrected right away; if not they will continue and could venture far from our homes.

When this occurs, it's not surprising that children are expelled or suspended from school for being disobedient. Or they might receive a traffic ticket for not obeying a traffic sign. Or more seriously, they could be arrested for driving under the influence of alcohol.

Teaching our children to be obedient is serious business; something not to be taken lightly.

Recently, I was watching the news surrounding the George Floyd murder. For those of you not familiar with the case...this incident involved the killing of George Floyd, a Black man, by four white police officers in Minneapolis, Minnesota. Although Floyd had been handcuffed behind his back and pushed to the ground, one officer held him down by placing his knee against his neck; while the other two officers pushed their knees on his back; the fourth officer stood watching. The police held Floyd down for 8 minutes and 46 seconds in spite of his cries that he could not breathe. Their excessive actions caused Floyd's death.

From all accounts, Floyd died on the street while the police had their knees on his neck and back which hampered the flow of oxygen and blood to his lungs and brain.

It's apparent that the officers did not obey the rules set forth by the police force. They were not acting in self- defense. How do I know this? I know this because they were immediately fired from their jobs and subsequently charged with murder. These officers were not only disobedient to the rules of law, but they also had no respect for or valued the life of a fellow human being.

One has to wonder what type of upbringing these officers received. Were they brought up in a God- fearing household; one that relied on God's teachings? I seriously doubt it. For if they did, there is no way that they could have committed such a senseless, non-provoked murder.

Keep in mind, not only did they disobey rules, but they broke one of the Ten Commandments, "Thou shall not kill". Even the officer who stood back and did nothing was comparable to the actions that caused the death. Death by omission. To do nothing and allow the act to continue knowing it was wrong was just as bad as having his knee on Mr. Floyd's neck.

As parents, we must not only be concerned about the present, but we must also be mindful of the future. Our present actions toward our children will dictate their future because our teachings, or lack of, will have direct influence on their adult lives. If we don't discipline them and teach them to be obedient now, then don't be surprised when they are disobedient as adults. Let's always remember *Proverbs 22:15, "'Foolishness is bound in the heart of a child: but the rod of correction shall drive it far from him."*

Other Obedience Related Scripture

John 14:15 - *If ye love me, keep my commandments*

1 Peter 1:14 - *As obedient children, not fashioning yourselves according to the former lusts in your ignorance:*

1 John 5:3 - *For this is the love of God, that we keep his commandments: and his commandments are not grievous.*

Exodus 23:22 - *But if thou shalt indeed obey his voice, and do all that I speak; then I will be an enemy unto thine enemies, and an adversary unto thine adversaries.*

Respectful

Parents, be ever so mindful of what you say and what you do around your children. As parents you must always set a good example for your children. Demonstrate respect. *Matthew 7:12 "Therefore, all things whatsoever ye that men should do to you, do ye even so to."* However, in spite of our best intentions, we are human and subject to making mistakes ourselves.

Never forget that children emulate others (family members, teachers, friends) and most often they emulate their parents. If you curse; they might follow suit. If you scream and yell at one another; they are likely to scream and yell if they are upset. If you are disrespectful to someone; they might show disrespect to others as well. Therefore, as parents you must be the model that you want your children to become.

Consequently, when things happen and we make a mistake, we must admit to that mistake and apologize. It's important to tell children that it's ok to make a mistake; that you might be wrong about something. At some point, everyone makes mistakes. But, it is important to admit that mistake and apologize for it. Apologies show children that you respect their feelings and feel sorry for your behavior.

I know that sometimes we might forget, but it's essential to exhibit good manners by using words such as "please", "thank you", "excuse me". Using such words illustrate that you are aware of the feelings of others and show respectful demeanor towards them.

Children hear you exhibiting good manners; they too will learn to follow suit. And of course, it's always good to speak to your children about using positive words and always being polite.

Have you ever been at a gathering and a friend or someone you know enters the room and says nothing? No greeting (Hi, how's everyone, good afternoon) It's not only rude but disrespectful. I was always taught that when you enter a room, you are to acknowledge; not wait for someone who is already in the room to acknowledge you. Teach your children to acknowledge people.

A show of respect is not a difficult task to obtain. Have you ever been on a crowded city bus or subway and observed teenagers sitting while an elderly man or woman is standing? The teens ignore the standing elderly; continue to enjoy their ride, sitting comfortably. But, then one of the teens spots the elderly person and offer his seat. That's s a show of respect for the elderly. Perhaps growing up that teen observed his parent or another individual carry out the same good deed.

******

I have many fond memories growing up in North Carolina, many of which center around the respect that men showed towards the women in our small town. It was common to see a group of men standing on the street engaged in vibrant conversation. However, if a woman passed them, they would stop talking, tip their hats, and give a cheerful greeting.

However, sad to say, but rarely do I see such respectful behavior now days.

******

Aretha Franklin's "Respect" gained popularity in the '70's but is still enjoyed by many today. In the song all she's asking for is a little R-E-S-P-E-C-T. So, in our everyday travels, can't we ask for the same, but also give the same. Set the example.

For many years, I've always put into practice the Golden Rule – "do unto others as you would have them do unto you". Isn't that exactly what God teaches us in *Galatians 5"14 For all the law is fulfilled in one word, even in this; Thou shalt love thy neighbour as thyself."*

Other Respect Related Scripture

Matthew 7:12 - *Therefore all things whatsoever ye would that men should do to you, do ye even so to them: for this is the law and the prophets.*

Romans 12:10 - *[Be] kindly affectioned one to another with brotherly love; in honour preferring one another*

Philippians 2:3 - *[Let] nothing [be done] through strife or vainglory; but in lowliness of mind let each esteem other better than themselves.*

1 Peter 2:17 - *Honour all [men]. Love the brotherhood. Fear God. Honour the king.*

Titus 2:7 - *In all things shewing thyself a pattern of good works: in doctrine [shewing] uncorruptness, gravity, sincerity,*

Humbleness

My mind immediately goes back to two of our former presidents: Jimmy Carter and Barack Obama. These men exemplified humility in every sense of the word. Their efforts were done out of love and compassion for others. Being humble means putting yourself in the background; putting others in the forefront. Doing for others without expecting recognition.

For more than 35 years, former President Jimmy Carter and his wife Rosalynn Carter have been dedicated to the mission of Habitat for Humanity, an organization that renovates or builds new housing for the less fortunate. They have not only been strong advocates and avid fundraisers for the organization, but also have volunteered and worked along side others to build.

How many of us know someone who is 95 plus years old and physically on the job site constructing houses? Few I can imagine. But, former President and Mrs. Carter's show of care, dedication, fortitude, compassion, and love are evidence of their humility.

Likewise, throughout his presidency, former President Barack Obama illustrated humility and love of mankind. One such example occurred when he was giving a television address after the Sandy Hook mass shooting. Standing on the podium with potentially thousands of television viewers watching, he wiped away tears. These were tears of compassion for the children who were the victims of a senseless murder.

His humility was also demonstrated during the funeral of a pastor gunned down in a senseless church murder in Charleston, SC. He concluded his eulogy by singing Amazing Grace. The President was gracefully demonstrating that although he was President of the United States and the most powerful man in the world, he was still "one of them"—not better or worse. He was just a member of the congregation giving respect to a fellow American.

In both instances, the President showed his humility—a noteworthy attribute that all should strive to attain. *Proverbs 11:12 : When pride comes, then comes disgrace, but with the humble is wisdom. (Micah 6:8). Jesus often spoke of humility, saying " and he hath showed thee, O man what is good and what does the Lord require of thee, but to do justly, and to love mercy, and to walk humbly with thy God."*

During both of their presidencies, Jimmy Carter and Barack Obama did much for the American people. They never boasted or bragged- a sign of humility. Those who are humble do not boast or brag; do not indulge in "self". They get inner fulfillment out of their desire to do whatever they can do help others.

That's what's being humble is all about: being respectful, kindhearted, compassionate, giving. One who is humble will demonstrate these qualities; will think of others, do not rely on praise from others. So, if our children can readily see these qualities in us and we consistently teach them God's word, then their humbleness; their humility will become evident.

Show by example. Give them opportunity to display the talents, the gifts that God has given them. Let them experience self-fulfillment that comes with doing for others. Compassion, love, giving, selflessness are all wrapped up in being humble. *Matthew 23:12 says, "And whosoever shall exalt himself shall be abased, and he that shall humble himself shall be exalted." In Mathew 18:4 our Savior taught us "Whosoever therefore shall humble himself as this little child, the same is greatest in the kingdom of heaven."*

Other Humbleness Related Scripture

<u>***Philippians 2:3-11***</u> - *[Let] nothing [be done] through strife or vainglory; but in lowliness of mind let each esteem other better than themselves.*

<u>***James 4:6***</u> - *But he giveth more grace. Wherefore he saith, God resisteth the proud, but giveth grace unto the humble.*

<u>***Proverbs 22:4***</u> - *By humility [and] the fear of the LORD [are] riches, and honour, and life*

<u>***1 Peter 5:6***</u> - *Humble yourselves therefore under the mighty hand of God, that he may exalt you in due t*

<u>Caring/Kindness</u>

The development of kindness and caring is crucial for our children's growth and development. These are characteristics that will help them to build and keep friendships and understand feelings of others. A show of kindness and caring builds an emotional connection with those that they are around.

I attempt to live by that Golden Rule: do unto others as you would have them do unto you, A kind word; a smile; a helping hand; a gentle touch; a warm hello –demonstrates kindness. Children are attentive to our actions. Again, be the role model.

******

We see actions of kindness and caring daily.

Our nation- the world- is currently plagued with the dreadful coronavirus pandemic. But, among all the suffering and death, we see many young people spending time making protective face masks for the medical staff and other frontline workers fighting to combat this evil. Instead of watching TV or playing video games, these young people chose to set aside a portion of their day to extend a helping hand to others. Caring means thinking of and doing for others. Also, think about the hundreds of people who organize and give out food every day at the food banks throughout our country. People coming together to help others in a time of crisis.

They are all followers of God's word. ***John 13:34-35*** - *A new commandment I give unto you, That ye love one another; as I have loved you, that ye also love one another.*

When I was a teen, and had worked and bought my first car, there were many times when I would take some of my elderly neighbors to the store to buy grocery or for general shopping. I never charged them anything. I did it out of the kindness of my heart.

None of us in my community had a lot of money, but we helped one another whenever possible. My parents had instilled in my siblings and me to help others. This is what they expected, and this is what God expects of His children.

I remember so many times when my mother would ask me to sit with some of the elderly in our community when they were alone. I would sometimes read to them, talk to them, listen to them, and do small chores for them. This was a time when I not only provided comfort to them, but this was also a way of letting them know that the community cared about their safety and well- being. *1Peter5:5 says, "Likewise, you who are younger, be subject to the elders. Clothe yourselves, all of you, with humility toward one another, for "God opposes the proud but gives grace to the humble."*

That characteristic of caring for and being kind

to others remain a part of me to this day. Remember at the beginning of this book, I expressed my desire to become a medical doctor –one caring for the sick. Well, I did not become a medical doctor, but I did become a doctor of sorts –a minister --one dedicated to caring for and saving souls of my fellow man.

******

I currently live in a racially mixed community; a community filled with folk of all ages; many children and young adults. I get very concerned though when I see so many of the children congregating on the streets well into the wee hours of the night unsupervised. They have so much freedom on their hands; so much time to get into mischief; unlimited opportunity to do something unlawful.

One day, I decided to visit the homes of many of those in my community. My objective was to see if I could get some of them to attend our church services. I was surprised at the number of parents and children who were willing to come. I immediately arranged to get the church bus to pick up and take them to Sunday services.

I was so excited, but that excitement soon faded because that first Sunday morning, no one showed up at the pickup point. No one showed up the next Sunday or the next or the next. Yes, I was discouraged; however, I will not give up; for, I believe, that on one Sunday morning someone will eventually show up.

That's one thing that my parents taught me: don't give up. Keep trying and you will succeed. Right now, my success is knowing that I'm doing all that I can to show others that I care about them and am expressing God's love for them. That self-satisfaction and fulfillment is enough for me at present.

I continually try to *follow Galatians5:10 which states,"As we have therefore opportunity, let us do good into all men, especially unto them who are of the household of faith."*

As our children were growing up, my wife and I raised them to be loving, caring, respective, and helpful to others. We introduced them to the church when they were just babies and taught them of God's love and his blessings. We were always filled with much pride when we saw our children interacting with other children, people in the community, and at church –exhibiting honesty, respect, and kindness.

Their teachers and school principals always

complemented them on their conduct in school; helping other classmates when needed and just exhibiting acts of kindness. We taught our children to be grateful of God's goodness, to be thankful, and to be givers to the less fortunate. Children will emulate, will follow your lead.

Other Scripture Related to Caring/Kindness

Philippians 2:4 - *Look not every man on his own things, but every man also on the things of others.*

Ephesians 4:32 - *And be ye kind one to another, tenderhearted, forgiving one another, even as God for Christ's sake hath forgiven you.*

1 John 3:17-18 - *But whoso hath this world's good, and seeth his brother have need..."*

Part 4
Possible Effects of Sparing the Rod (Not Disciplining)

Some parents may not want to discipline their children for various reasons. Some may want to avoid conflict. Some may not know the best way to discipline. Others may have had unpleasant disciplinary experiences themselves growing up and don't want their children to be subjected to similar outcomes. The list goes on.

But when parents do not discipline, children are left to make decisions on their own. Sometimes, they make the wrong decisions resulting in behavior that could have drastic negative effects on their lives. *Proverbs 22:15* *tells us that "Foolishness is bound up in the heart of a child; the rod of discipline will remove it far from him."*

We just shared potential characteristics that could result when children are disciplined. Now, let's look at potential characteristics that could result when children are not disciplined.

These include, but not limited to: disobedience, lack of identity, unkind/inhumane, arrogant (narcissistic), dishonesty, disrespectful.

Disobedience

I think that I can safely say that all parents have faced the challenge of a disobedient child. Consider the number of times that you have told your children not to go outdoors without their hat and gloves, but they do anyway. Or you told them to clean their rooms, but return only to find the room still not cleaned. Can you even count the number of times they were told to do their homework before watching TV; but later find that they not only watched TV, but their homework was still incomplete? These occurrences might seem minor, but if not corrected, these types of behaviors could lead to more serious situations. <u>*Colossians 3:20*</u> *states, "Children, obey your parents in all things, for this is pleasing unto the Lord."*

"Nip disobedience in the bud." Let children know that consequences come with being disobedient. If they misbehave, they will be disciplined in some manner. No TV or no attending the ball game. If they break school rules, there will be detention or suspension. For teens, if they drive above the speed limits, there's a possibility of a fine. If they break the law, there is a possibility of going to jail.

A child's disobedience is not to be tolerated. *Proverbs 19:18 "Chasten thy son while there is hope and let not thy soul spare for his crying." Proverbs 30:17-18 goes on to say, 'Correct thy son, and he shall give delight unto thy soul. Where there is no vision, the people perish: but he that keepeth the law, happy is he."*

In all of these scriptures there comes teachings on how to raise your children so that they may become obedient, respectful young adults. Although we speak in detail of the "rod" this is where we can see that the "rod" can come in many forms. The key is to be consistent with the discipline and make sure the child understands the reason behind the discipline. By teaching them that there are consequences to every bad behavior, you hope to save them from some of the more harsh outcomes that those in the world may bestow on them from breaking the rules.

Children are to *"Honor thy father and thy mother: that thy days may be long upon land which the Lord thy God giveth thee. (Exodus 20:12)* Other scripture state *"Thou shalt not kill. Thou shall not commit adultery. Thou shalt not steal. Thou shalt not bear false witness against thy neighour." (Exodus 20:13-16)*

Obedience means being in alignment with the Word and with that alignment it is promised by the Word to bring blessings. Disobedience brings forth punishment and shame.

Follow God's words. Teach and guide your

children; that's what a responsible, loving parent does.

Other Disobedience Related Scripture

James 1:14-15 - *But every man is tempted, when he is drawn away of his own lust, and enticed.*
John 14:15 - *If ye love me, keep my commandments.*

2 Timothy 3:1-7 - *This know also, that in the last days perilous times shall come.*
Romans 6:23 - *For the wages of sin [is] death; but the gift of God [is] eternal life through Jesus Christ our Lord.*

Lack of Identity

Today's youth can be influenced by many different avenues from television, movies, social media to their peers as well as adults to include parents, family, and friends. How they view themselves and those whom they view as role models play a vital part in their grow and development. Some are drawn towards the seemingly glamorous lifestyle of models or movie stars or secular singers.

Simply speaking, some youth may have difficulty identifying just who they are. They might find fault in themselves because of their physical appearance or how they talk or where they live or the types of clothes they wear.

Do you recall a few years back when many teens sort to look like Michael Jackson? Some bought outfits or wore their hair similar to his. That wasn't so bad, but then there were those who took it to the extreme by having plastic surgery. They wanted their nose shaped like his or their cheek bones or their skin color to be similar as well.

What about those youth who resort to augmenting their breasts or butts by injecting foreign elements into their bodies? Many times, parents agree for these changes to be made instead of encouraging their children to love themselves and not take the chance of doing harm to their bodies.

Growing up can be hard, full of indecisiveness, not knowing what to do or who to follow. Parent guidance is essential and when it is not provided, wrong choices can be made.

Because of my ministry, I often talk with,

counsel youths coming from various home settings.

In my sessions, I have found it to be evident that everyone wants to be a part of something. Something that offers some form of satisfaction and gives them a sense of belonging.

Because of this sense of belonging, often times, we find children drawn into street gangs; gangs terrorizing the neighborhood, robbing stores and other businesses; gang members beating up and killing other gang members or everyday citizens.

Why do you think this occurs? Apparently, there's something lacking in the home environment. That show of love and affection and belonging have to be present at all times. These coupled with discipline will help the children avoid making wrong decisions such as joining a gang and ending up in prison or even worse... dead.

******

One of the saddest feelings that has ever come over me is when I attend a funeral and officials of the federal authority or police bring in a prisoner in handcuffs and shackles to view the body of a parent.

As I watch the prisoner, I wonder how he feels and if some of the following thoughts are going through his mind:

I was a child and you did not teach me right from wrong.
I was a child and you let me have my way; you did not try to correct me.
I was a child and yet you didn't make me go to church with you so I could also learn about the goodness of Jesus Christ.
I was a child and you did not punish me for skipping school.
I was a child and could have had a good education and a good life if I had been trained properly.
I was a child not raised with good Godly training and now the rest of my life is destroyed and all I look forward to now is Spending the rest of my life in prison.
I was a child and if I could be a child again, I would never make these mistakes again.
I was a child who needed to be raised and you didn't. I put the blame on you, my parents.

Powerful statements!

I also wonder what the other funeral attendees

think and perhaps hoping that they would not experience a similar situation. I have witnessed this too often and I imagine there has to be some shame somewhere. *"The rod and reproof give wisdom, but a child let to himself bringeth his mother to shame." Proverbs 29:1*

So many choices, so many decisions that our children have to make.

******

Our communities are inundated with alcohol and recreational drugs . It's a parent's job to use love and experience to correct mistakes and poor choices that our children make. As such, parents must not only educate our children to the ills of taking either drugs or alcohol, but also stress to *them "... ye are the temple of God, and that the Spirit of God dwelleth in you..."(Corinthians 3:16-17).* As a temple of God, we must not ingest anything that will cause harm to our body (the temple).

But, without guidance it is not surprising to know that children as young as 7 or 8 years old use drugs and/or alcohol. At this age, they are very vulnerable and can be easily influenced and anxious to be a part of the "group". That's why parents must constantly and consistently talk with them, guide them, show them how these drugs can have adverse effects not only on their body but also on their lives. That training must teach them how to say "NO".

We see from the following chart that alcohol and marijuana use is alive and well among our teens. As you will note, this data only represent a segment of our youth. It does not even consider those younger than 12th graders.

ALCOHOL
58% of 12th graders tried alcohol 6% drove after drinking 16% rode in a car of someone who had been drinking
MARIJUANA
16% of 12th graders have used in a 30- day period 10% of high schoolers making A's use; while 48% earning D's and F's use

Based on The Recovery Village article statistics

******

During my ministry, I recall many instances when other church members and I would go through our community providing help to those who were drug and alcohol abusers. These individuals were homeless, needing medical care, food, clothing, and shelter. Despite their circumstance, many did not want to or could not change their addiction. They listened to us as we spoke to them of God's love. They took the literature that we disseminated. They accepted the food and clothing we gave. But few changed their habits.

Thou this was the case, we followed God's word as is written in Matthew 5:16 *"In the same way, let your light shine before others, so that they may see your good works and give glory to your Father who is in heaven." Hebrews 13:16 "And do not forget to do good and to share with others, for with such sacrifices God is pleased."*

Likewise, parents must do whatever is necessary to follow God's word and be a guide for their children. Surely no parent wants his child to be addicted to drugs and alcohol and be subject to the ills of that addiction; such as the ones who become homeless dependent upon others for survivor. But, that could very well happen if parents are not obedient and teach children that they are not to defy God's temple.

When a child hasn't been able to create a

positive self-image (identity) they look to others, like gangs to create it for them. They often take on the identity of others to fit in, I.E. tough guy role. When a parent builds positive self- identity within their child, they allow them to grow and love who they are instead of trying to find their identity with others.

Other Lack of Identity Related Scripture

Genesis 1:27 - *So God created man in his [own] image, in the image of God created he him; male and female created he them*

Jeremiah 1:5 - *Before I formed thee in the belly I knew thee; and before thou camest forth out of the womb I sanctified thee, [and] I ordained thee a prophet unto the nations.*

2 Corinthians 5:17 - *Therefore if any man [be] in Christ, [he is] a new creature: old things are passed away; behold, all things are become new.*

1 Corinthians 12:27 - *Now ye are the body of Christ, and members in particular.*

Unkind/ Inhumane

It goes without saying that children's early life experiences, set the stage for how they will develop the ability to think, feel, trust, and relate to others. What takes place in the home, those early experiences will impact our children and determine what type of adults they will become.

Our children are what we make them. Sounds like a monumental task. But, God gives us all the guidance that we need to accomplish that task. *Psalm 11:5* *"The LORD tests the righteous, but his soul hates the wicked and the one who loves violence."*

No, parenting is not easy. It requires a lot of hard work. But, unfortunately, sometimes regardless of how hard we try to put into practice what we view as good parenting skills, sometimes our children may exhibit violent or abusive behavior. When this happens, they must be held accountable every time for those behaviors. They must realize that there are consequences for their actions, and make sure those consequences (disciplinary actions) are set up as learning experiences. You want the consequence to teach your child what to do differently next time.

Holding children accountable for their actions is essential for them to mature as responsible adults. So, if your child purposely breaks his sister's doll because he is angry with her, then he must know that there are consequences for his behavior. And as a parent, you must determine what disciplinary measures to take that will teach the child that that type behavior is unacceptable, that there are alternative ways of handling anger. *Ephesians 6:1:"Children, obey your parents in the Lord, for this is right*."

******

Often, we read or hear about numerous cases of bullying in our neighborhoods, schools, and even in our homes. Combating this societal evil, starts in the home. When parents discover that their child is bullying another child they need to correct that situation and make it known that bullying is wrong and will not be tolerated. This means in the home as well as outside the home. If not addressed, this issue can escalate and lead to situations more serious than teasing or name calling.

Recently, the news carried an incident surrounding a female adolescent, a victim of bullying, who died after a fight with another classmate. Another story reported an 8 -year old who committed suicide because he was a victim of bullying. So, when parents discover any aspects of bullying behavior, they need to step in and stop this destructive behavior.

Interesting Facts on Bullying

- Students who experience bullying are at increased risk for poor school adjustment, sleep difficulties, anxiety, and depression (**Center for Disease Control, 2015**).
- Students who are both targets of bullying and engage in bullying behavior are at greater risk for both mental health and behavior problems than students who only bully or are only bullied (**Center for Disease Control, 2015**).
- Students who bully others, are bullied, or witness bullying are more likely to report high levels of suicide-related behavior than students who report no involvement in bullying (**Center for Disease Control, 2014**).

******

Of equal importance, a household should be free of violent behavior. We all know that violence can escalate from arguments, to fighting, to bodily harm. *Colossians 3:21" Fathers, provoke not your children [to anger], lest they be discouraged."* So we want to always be in position of maintaining some semblance of peace and harmony in the home.

The father has the responsibility for establishing the framework with which the child is to follow in the home. The mother's discipline is an extension of the father's established rules and regulations. Therefore, in order for peace and calm to exist in the household, then the parents must set example. By nature, children often mimic their parents. If they observe their parents exhibiting violent behavior –yelling, screaming, fighting -- they may also do the same. In essence, parents need to be a role model for their children and set the example by doing what is good and showing integrity and seriousness.

******

Let's be mindful that when God and His teachings are absent from the home, oftentimes children can be the victims of neglect and abuse. As parents, your job is to care for your children. Kathleen M. Heide, etal states, " between 1976 and 1999 less than 25% of biological mothers and fathers slain were killed by juveniles under age eighteen." Most of these killing were attributed to juveniles experiencing physical, mental, or sexual abuse.

Neglect and abuse fall outside of the boundaries of parenthood. Neglect and abuse can have devastating long-term effects on their lives. Ephesians 6:4 *"Fathers, do not provoke your children to anger, but bring them up in the discipline and instruction of the Lord."*

How often do we read or hear of situations in which abused children and young adults have murdered their parents? As shocking as it sounds, it does happen time and time again. Mark 13:12 *"Now the brother shall betray the brother to death, and the father the son, and children shall rise up against parents, and shall cause them to be put to death."*

******

As unbelievable as it is with children murdering their parents for whatever reason, it is also disturbing to know that home abuse could extend beyond the home and result in school killings. Much research has been conducted to determine why this occurs. "School shooters often have had stressful conditions at home or school (Levin & Madfis, 2009). Leary, Kowalski, Smith, and Phillips (2003) found that school shooters felt chronic rejection in 13 of the 15 school shooting incidents that they analyzed. The Chronic Strain at home appears to be reflected in the fact that some school shooters kill their parents or other members of their family prior to the shooting." (Mendoza, 2002)

Further, Peterson and Densley (2019) assert that school shooters typically have four things in common: "They suffered early-childhood trauma and exposure to violence at a young age. They were angry or despondent over a recent event, resulting in feelings of suicidality."

******

Time has definitely brought about drastic unbelievable change. During my youth, I never heard of any school shootings. In my household, my parents were obedient to God's word and taught us to be obedient as well. Because we attended church services and Bible study regularly, we were very familiar with one of the Ten Commandments which clearly states *"Thou shalt not kill", (Exodus 20:13).* I believe that many of the problems that exist today are a direct result of families and children not being guided by God's word.

It is mind boggling how accessible guns are today. And quite unbelievable the types of guns that children can get. As a child, I believe that the only type of gun in our house and our neighbors' homes were a shot gun and/or rifle that were used mainly for hunting. Some folk may have had pistols. But, no child bought a gun to school and definitely there were no mass school killings that I ever heard of.

******

I'm sure the children who were guilty of school shootings showed symptoms that something was wrong. Perhaps there were signs of depression, or they may have been victims of bullying. There could have been any number of clues. As parents, we must be observant and must listen to our children, support them, give them the help that they need.

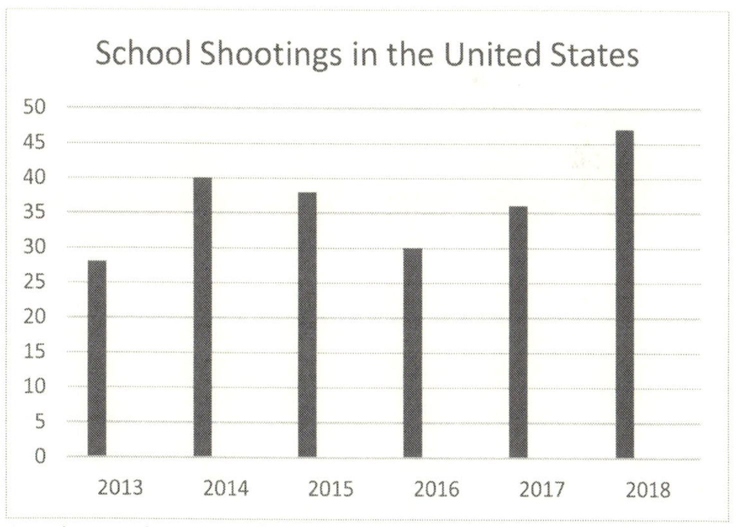

Attacks on others using firearms on school grounds in the U.S.
Source: Everytown for Gun Safety Support Fund.

Proverbs 22: 6 says" Train up a child in the way he should go and when he is old, he will not depart from it." It is the parents' duty to guide the child and teach him that as a child of God, he is to learn and carry out everything that is pleasing to God.

Perhaps God's teachings were not an integral part of these young folks' lives. Conceivably, if they were, then the numerous shootings that have occurred might have been avoided.

But, it is extremely depressing to know that teenagers and elementary aged students commit many of the school shootings.

I would be remiss if I did not mention the fact that our laws have seemingly made it somewhat easy for firearms to be attainable. They are sold not only at gun stores, but also at trade shows. These firearms can range from rifles to shot guns to pistols to automatic high-power assault weapons which are designed for military use.

I cannot understand why our government allows high power assault weapons to be sold to the general public. In many instances, assault weapons have been used in school shootings. Consequently, I blame our federal and local governments as well as the National Rifle Association (NRA) for the ease with which these firearms and be acquired and their horrific results.

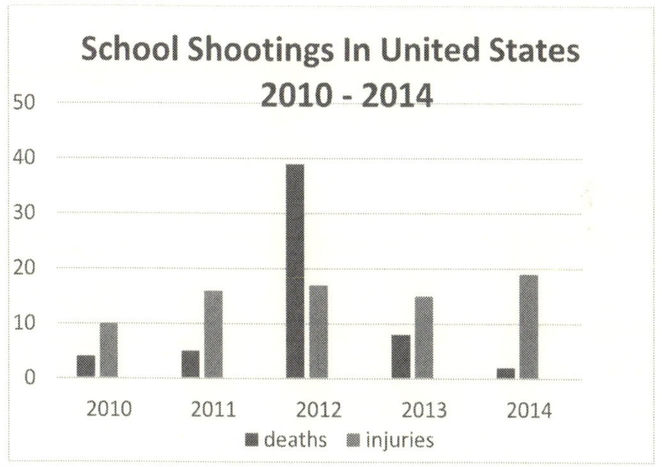

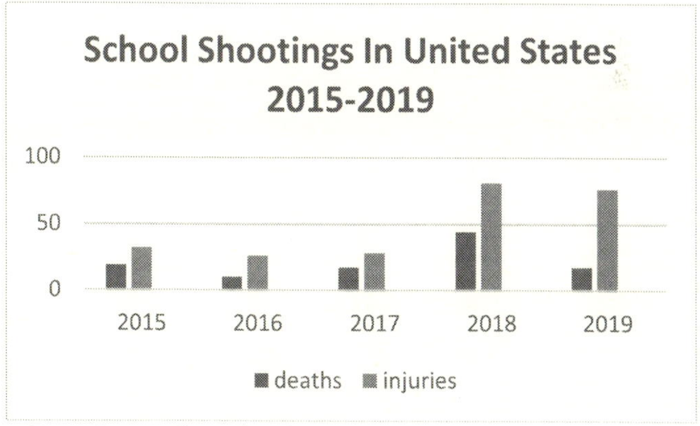

Based on Wikipedia data

It's astounding as we review the two charts above, from 2010 – 2019, a total of 178 people were killed as a result of school shootings and

337 were injured. Incredible!

Unfortunately, it appears that shootings have become an intricate part of our lives. That's why it is crucial for parents to step up and talk to their children (at an early age) about God and His expectations of His children. Take them to church, read the Bible. Get them acquainted with God and His teachings.

We pray for peace and guidance, but when a crisis such as this continues, we sometimes question if God hears those prayers. But, his Word says, *"I have heard thy prayer and seen thy tears: Behold I will heal thee." (2Kings 20:5)*

So regardless of the storms of life that we endure, know that God hears our prayers and sees our tears. Prayer is powerful and can give us peace within our hearts and enable us to move forward and face and weather these storms. There is hope!

Exodus20:9 simply says, "You shall not murder."

Other Scripture Related To Being Unkind

Isaiah 10:1-2 Woe to those who enact evil statutes. And to those who constantly record unjust decisions, So as to deprive the needy of justice..."

Ezekiel 45:9 'Thus says the Lord God, "Enough, you princes of Israel; put away violence and destruction, and practice justice and righteousness..."

Exodus 22:21 "You shall not wrong a stranger or oppress him, for you were strangers in the land of Egypt.

Exodus 23:9 "You shall not oppress a stranger, since you yourselves know the feelings of a stranger, for you also were strangers in the land of Egypt.

Zechariah 7:10 and do not oppress the widow or the orphan, the stranger or the poor; and do not devise evil in your hearts against one another.

Arrogant/ Narcissistic

In my daily walk, I try not to be critical of others, but try to focus on the good. Unfortunately, in all honesty, this can be difficult when my paths cross so many folk who care only for themselves, are arrogant, narcissistic, lack sensitivity, put themselves above others, and are selfish.

Let me take a moment to digress and share this interesting story with you. I was acquainted with this young couple who originally lived in North Carolina, not far from where I was reared. Many years ago, this couple moved from North Carolina to Northern Virginia. The husband, whom I will refer to as Sam was a womanizer; he often cheated on his wife, whom I will refer to as Beth. Soon after moving to Virginia, Sam started dating a young lady who soon found herself pregnant.

After the baby was born, Sam somehow managed to get custody of the child, whom we will refer to as Junior. Beth welcomed Junior into the family and treated him as her own. Beth and Sam spoiled Junior, giving him anything that he wanted. He was never corrected when he was disobedient; never disciplined in any manner—regardless of what he said or did.

When Junior was a toddler, Sam would always bring snacks home for him; snacks that were never shared with any other children who might have been in the household. You see, Beth took care of children in the neighborhood while their parents worked.

Sometimes during the day, Beth would give Junior the goodies while the other children looked on; never sharing with the children. So, Junior was never taught to "do unto others as you would have them do unto you".

Junior was very unruly, always disobeying his parents if he couldn't get his way. Beth and Sam never disciplined him during his development; whatever he wanted, he got. Junior showed his parents no respect. He would yell at them; talk back to them; throw temper tantrums at home and in public. It mattered not. So again, Junior was never taught to honor his mother and father nor to respect others or even care about them or their opinions.

Junior's behavior was literally affecting both Sam's and Beth's health. Sam developed a heart condition. One Sunday, Sam and Junior were in church when tragedy struck. Sam had a heart attack and died with Junior sitting beside him on the church's pew. Junior was around 8 or 9 years old.

After Sam's passing, Beth still did nothing to correct Junior's behavior. He was in total control of the household. If he wanted something from the store, 12 o'clock at night, he would make his mother go out to the store and get whatever he wanted. Beth would get up out of her bed and go to the store to get ice cream or soda or candy, whatever darling Junior wanted.

By always yielding to his demands, Beth was telling Junior that his demands would be met regardless of the constraints or feelings of others. He would always get what he wanted.

It didn't matter if she were sick; if it was cold, rainy, snowing; she would go to satisfy Junior's every desire. It's shameful to say, but at 12 years old, Junior was still throwing temper tantrums. If he and his mother were at the store and she didn't have enough money to get everything he wanted, he would lie length wise in the car seat so that she could not get behind the steering wheel. Beth would always have to call a male family member to come down to the store to make Junior move so that she could drive home.

Totally ridiculous. But, true. This would happen each and every time they went shopping.

One day at the grocery store, Beth didn't have money to get something that Junior wanted. Well, we know what happened, Junior threw a tantrum in the car. This time, Beth got so upset she ended up having a heart attack and died on the spot.

After Beth's death, Junior was sent to live with his grandmother. For years, I didn't hear about Junior. But, I do know when he became of age, he joined the United States Army. It was after he had been in the Army for a few years that he paid me a visit. To my surprise, he was respectful and well mannered. During our conversation, he expressed that he wished he had been more respectful to his parents during his youth.

No doubt, even years after their passing, he was still troubled by his behavior towards his parents. But on the bright side, we can also see what happens when discipline steps into the picture. I don't know if Junior's grandmother disciplined him; but I do know that the Army did; for, discipline is the foundation of the military. *Proverbs 22:6 says,"Teach children how they should live, and they will remember it all their life."*

During Junior's childhood, his parents spared the rod. With every tantrum, every demand, every disrespectful behavior, Junior was crying out for help from his parents. He was crying out for discipline, but his parents did not hear his cry. They did not follow God's word; so subsequently, they suffered the consequences. Junior took over; in essence, he was saying "since you did not train me, I will train you". And that's just what he did. He trained them to do whatever he wanted, whenever he wanted.

******

I cannot end this section without mentioning the rhetoric and self-gratification of some of our public officials, and I wonder how in the world they were ever elected. Often, they seek public support, admiration, and acknowledgement on everything they do and say. Behavior that is totally against God's teachings.

Romans 12:3 *" For I say, through the grace given unto me, to every man that is among you, not to* *think [of himself] more highly than he ought to think; but to think soberly, according as God hath dealt to every man the measure of faith."*

Furthermore, it's sad for me to say, that our current president, Donald Trump, demonstrates such characteristics. In his viewpoint, he is always right and whoever disagrees with him could find themselves without a job. He's quick to fire or make negative comments toward those who oppose him. Twitter temper tantrums are his specialty.

It's sad to say that there are many Donald Trumps and Juniors today. Junior's story had a positive ending, but that might not be the case for other children who are not disciplined by their parents and grow up to be adults still throwing "temper tantrums" when they do not get everything they want or are not praised and given some sort of recognition with every act conducted.

Other Arrogance Related Scripture

Proverbs 8:13 - *The fear of the LORD [is] to hate evil: pride, and arrogancy, and the evil way, and the froward mouth, do I hate.*

Isaiah 13:11 - *And I will punish the world for [their] evil, and the wicked for their iniquity; and I will cause the arrogancy of the proud to cease, and will lay low the haughtiness of the terrible.*

Luke 18:9-14 - *And he spake this parable unto certain which trusted in themselves that they were righteous, and despised others: .*

1 Timothy 5:8 - *But if any provide not for his own, and specially for those of his own house, he hath denied the faith, and is worse than an infidel.*

Dishonesty

Colossians 3:9-10 – *"Lie not one to another, seeing that ye have put off the old man with his deeds."*

It's a shame to say, but we find dishonest people in almost every aspect of life. Let's start with the church, familiar ground. Dishonesty from the pulpit to the congregation. Yes, I said it: the pulpit.

Just the other day, I saw a TV commercial with this minister talking about "bottled miracle water". He advocates if you drink this miracle water, all sorts of good things will come to past – money, new homes, jobs, the list goes on. Then, to validate his claims, several people who have had the pleasure of drinking this miracle water have all types of wondrous things happening in their lives. One woman received $12,000, another, $50,000, another cured from some deadly illness, and another and another. I do not believe any of it.

Remember Jim Jones? Preacher and faith healer who became cult leader. God says beware of false prophets. Seemingly, Jim Jones' followers didn't follow God's warnings but chose to follow Jim Jones which led to their eventual deaths.

Still looking within the church, believe it or not, but there are some deacons or trustees who dip into the collection plates too. Hard to believe, but it happens time and time again. Dishonesty at play. Tell me, where is their religious faith when they stoop so low as to steal from the church?

Moving on.

******

In the time of the world COVID-19 pandemic, there are scammers out to benefit: big businesses and corporations at the top of the list. Furthermore, I read an article recently where some folk were intercepting the U.S. mail and forging their name on Stimulus checks. Imagine stealing money from those in dire need.

Now, we surely can't leave out those who pose as being homeless, needing food and shelter. Some are legit, but many are not. At the end of the day, the fakers get into their luxury cars with their daily monetary gains and return to their suburban homes.

******

For the past 20 years, I have been a real estate agent in the Northern Virginia area. I've had the opportunity of meeting people from all walks of life: doctors, lawyers, construction workers, teachers, business owners—to name a few. Most I've found to be honest seeking bigger and or better housing in good neighborhoods. But, one couple will forever be memorable to me.

This couple had been married for several years

and had good employment and credit history. As their application was being investigated, we discovered that they were not whom they claimed to be. They had forged the names of the wife's parents. Luckily, this information was discovered, and the application was denied. This incident bothered me then and still bothers me now because I just cannot understand how anyone can try to take advantage of their parents in this manner.

How does this happen? Why so much dishonesty? Somewhere down the line, there was a gap in the parents' disciplinary techniques. Parents did not instill honesty. Perhaps a little lie was not corrected; so, it just mushroomed into bigger lies. Lies that eventually became a way of life. Sad, but oh so true.

******

But, all is not loss. We don't have to be taken in by these liars, these dishonest people, despite their claims; their smooth, convincing talk.

God has equipped us with a "sixth" sense; a warning sense: discernment. An inner feeling that you get when something is not quite right; something doesn't add up. God warns us, but we often don't heed his warnings. That's when we get taken in by these scammers (preachers and church folk included in this group). Listen to that sixth sense and disarm the dishonesty.

So, it goes without saying if parents taught their children to listen to their inner self, they too can decipher truth from dishonesty.

Other Dishonesty Related Scripture

Proverbs 20:17 - *Bread of deceit [is] sweet to a man; but afterwards his mouth shall be filled with gravel.*

Exodus 20:16 - *Thou shalt not bear false witness against thy neighbour.*

Proverbs 11:3 - *The integrity of the upright shall guide them: but the perverseness of transgressors shall destroy the*

Proverbs 16:28 - *A froward man soweth strife: and a whisperer separateth chief friends.*

Proverbs 11:1 - *A false balance [is] abomination to the LORD: but a just weight [is] his delight.*

Disrespectful

"To disrespect someone is to show a lack of respect, especially by saying impolite things to them or by acting rude or being offensive." (Webster) Nowadays it doesn't take much to observe children being disrespectful to their parents *Ephesians 6:1-3 says , "Children obey your parents in the Lord: for this is right. Honour thy father and mother which is the first commandment with promise; that it may be well with thee, and thou mayest live long on the earth."*

Children talking back to their parents are being disrespectful and not honoring them. Children being rude to their parents are being disrespectful and not honoring them. Children cursing their parents are being disrespectful and hot honoring them.

If this behavior is not corrected, then it is quite evident that the same type behavior can be observed outside of the home environment. How many times do we read about children talking back to school officials, or cursing someone, or calling someone out of their name? These unsavory behaviors fall back on the parent; for, it is the parents' duty to teach and guide.

Disrespectful actions go against scripture. Children are to respect their parents in every sense of the word. Parents are responsible for their being. They feed them, cloth them, provide for them, give them shelter, love them. Children must realize that their parents are on this earth but for a period of time; when they are gone—there are only memories. Children should cherish their parents.

But, I would be remiss if I did not say that if parents do not discipline their children when they are disrespectful, then the parents are being disobedient to God's word. *Proverbs 19:18* *"Discipline your son, for there is hope; do not set your heart on putting him to death.* *Proverbs 29:17* *"Discipline your son, and he will give you rest; he will give delight to your heart."*

Sometimes though, parents may do their best to discipline their children but somewhere in their children's growth and development something goes amiss. Let me give an example.

I have been acquainted with this family for many years. They are God fearing people who raised their children in the church and are advocate followers of God's words. In fact, I view this family as one of my closest friends.

Growing up, their children were well mannered, polite, and courteous. They were good students in school and never in trouble to my knowledge. During their youth, their parents disciplined them; taught them right from wrong, showed them much love and affection.

However, I was totally speechless not too long ago when the father confided in me about their home situation. He informed me that one of his daughters had grown to be most disrespectful and inconsiderate to both him and his wife. Case and point-- If his wife is watching a favorite gospel program and his daughter wants to watch another type program, she changes the channel without saying a word to her mother. To make matters worse if the father changes the channel back, then the daughter curses him. I was astounded hearing this. Total disrespect.

Unfortunately, this type of disrespect happens all the time and is widespread. We cannot forget that social media and television exposes our children to all types of situations. All it takes is a "click" and there's a pornographic scene or children yelling and screaming at an adult, or teens engaging in sexual behavior.

And, I'm sorry to say that in recent times, it is not surprising to see a police officer on the news hitting or kicking a woman who is peacefully demonstrating. This is very upsetting because many children look up to police officers; many want to grow up to become a policeman themselves. Police officers are role models to many children. So, what kind of message is being sent when a child sees a police officer – his role model- hitting a woman?

Let's forever be remined that children can be easily influenced by what they see and hear. That is why parents must constantly be on guard with everything their children do and with the types of friends they hang out with, what they experience in the neighborhood, and what they are watching on TV.

My friend had no idea what caused such a drastic change in his daughter's personality and was at his wits end trying to find a solution to the problem. When we as parents cannot solve the problem with our disciplinary techniques, then we might have to result to professional advice. Bottom line, we must parent regardless of how difficult the situation might be. Continue to seek out an effective disciplinary technique. If not, the negative behavior will continue and possibly get worst. But never forget to follow God's Word for the answer to any problem is there.

Other Disrespectful Related Scripture

Philippians 2:1-30 - *If [there be] therefore any consolation in Christ, if any comfort of love, if any fellowship of the Spirit, if any bowels and mercies,*

Proverbs 20:17 - *Bread of deceit [is] sweet to a man; but afterwards his mouth shall be filled with gravel.*

Colossians 3:9-10 - *Lie not one to another, seeing that ye have put off the old man with his deeds; .*

Proverbs 11:1 - *A false balance [is] abomination to the LORD: but a just weight [is] his delight.*

Hebrews 13:18 - *Pray for us: for we trust we have a good conscience, in all things willing to live honestly.*

Part 5
The Big Question?

Yes, the big question. How did we ever reach the point when a child could dare utter such words, "Since you didn't train me, now I will train you.? The answer could rest upon one thing or a combination of things. Let's consider a few possibilities.

Could the decision to remove prayer from schools have something to do with it? Seems unrelated? Well, let's see.

When I was in school, we began the school day with an opportunity to engage in silent prayer before beginning our regular school lessons. I'm sure many of you had the same opportunity. This moment of prayer gave us a time when we could come together and share a time of calm and set a positive mood for the school day. In a sense, it did enhance the probability and possibility for us to be respectful of each other and of the school officials. We associate God with respect, love, kindness. Therefore, in my opinion, prayer in school was a good thing. It had a positive influence on us and on our behavior. According to *Matthew 18:20, "For where two or three are gathered in my name, here am I among them."*

Over time, with a more diverse community arising in the United States and differences in religious beliefs, groups began to object to exercising prayer in school. In two landmark decisions – Engel v. Vitale on June 25, 1962, and Abington School District v. Schempp on June 17, 1963 – the Supreme Court declared school-sponsored prayer and Bible readings unconstitutional.

However, contrary to popular belief, the Supreme Court has never outlawed "prayer in schools." Students are free to pray alone or in groups, as long as such prayers are not disruptive and do not infringe upon the rights of others.

Although schools no longer encourage prayer in school, let's not forget that prayer begins at home. Growing up in a Christian household, we always said our prayers before going to bed and during other times of the day. My wife and I continue this practice as we reared our children. I'm sure you've had and still have similar experiences. If we teach our children to continually give thanks to God, it becomes a norm; prayer becomes a way of life. As believers of God, we can engage in never-ending conversation with Him. 1 Thessalonians 5:17 encourages us to "pray without ceasing" or to pray continually.

A ban on school prayer does not have to have a negative influence on our children's growth and development. Parents are to teach and show children the goodness of God. While riding in our cars or on public transportation; while taking a morning walk or jog; we can give thanks to God for the sunshine and rain that enables our fruits and vegetable to grow, for the beautiful flowers and trees. We can give thanks to God for our families; for our health and strength; for our jobs; for our peace of minds.

In essence, we can give thanks to God for so many things in our lives, regardless of where we are and what we are doing. We do not have to wait for some special occasion to do so. We do not have to wait until Thanksgiving dinner to go around the table and ask everyone what they are thankful for. That's something we can do every day at every meal.

Again, as parents, we are to set the standard. When we do so, there is less chance for our children to even think about making such a statement.

Could the statement, "since you didn't train me, now I will train you," have been influenced by the company that our children keep; or by the TV or movies that they view? A reasonable possibility. *2 Corinthians 6:14 says, "Do not be unequally yoked with unbelievers. For what partnership has righteousness with lawlessness? Or what fellowship has light with darkness?"*

That's why it's essential that we parent. And that we as parents must be in agreement with the manner in which we train our children. We set the limits. We teach them right from wrong.

It's important that we are always aware of who

our children befriend and the types of entertainment that they engage in. These are changing times and we must keep up with the times so that we can be informative and direct our children the way they should go.

" Foolishness is bound up in the heart of a child; the rod of discipline will remove it far from him." (Proverbs22:15).

Or could the statement, "since you did not train me, now I will train you," be a direct result of parents wanting to be their children's friends? How many of you have ever heard a parent state that their son or daughter is their best friend? Throughout their lifetime, your children will make many friends, but you as a parent is not one of them. God blessed your child with one mother and one father. Your role is to be a parent, not your child's friend.

Furthermore, friends are usually in the same age category. Friends share similar interests, like doing things together, etc. Oftentimes, friends will tell each other what they want to hear. Parents teach and guide; they share truths with their children. They set the stage for their children's growth and development.

Yes, in doing so, parents should and will have good, positive relationships with children. In building those positive relations, parents may and should go to the movies with their children or roller skate with them or have fun going to the pizza café'. In general, have fun with their children.

But, they are not their children's friend. They are their parents. Let's not confuse our children by putting ourselves on the same level as our children. Referring to them as your friend, does just that.

I will venture to say that if we PARENT, that is, be a positive role model for our children; teach and guide our children, then our children will not even think about saying 'since you didn't train me, then I will train you". Parents, be faithful and obedient to God's Word and carry out the role that our Heavenly Father has given – parent our children.

Part 6
A Final Look

God's plan for marriage and parenthood is evident in the Book of Genesis:1-28 with the creation of and union of Adam and Eve. The expressed purpose of this union was to bring forth children all of which would be born into sin, but with free will. This means that we have the free will to make choices surrounding our lives.

But because God is omnipotent and all knowing, he knew that man would need help in all aspects of life. He knew that when it came to raising children, we would need all the help that we could get. So, he provided us with guidelines for raising our children. Throughout this book, I have pointed out several scriptures that are found in the Bible which reference raising children.

Within the family structure, God says in Ephesians 6:4 that the father is to be the head of the household, setting the rules for the obedience of children. Any discipling done by the mother is an extension of the father's authority.

The art of parenthood could possibly be more effective, or even easier when the household has both father and mother who are on one accord—as was the intension of the Creator.

Throughout our marriage, my wife and I sort to be the parenting role model that God outlined in his Word. Our love and respect for one another was clearly evident to our children. And we, of course, extended those values to our children. We worked together, played together, prayed together. We showed our children that we cared about their interests by accompanying them to school ball games or various activities.

My girls liked to help their mother bake cookies, cakes, pies. And they both ended up being pretty good cooks. My boys on the other hand enjoyed going with me down to my TV shop. They loved to "tinker" as I, and eventually learned some valuable work skills as well.

As I look back, I don't believe I ever whipped my children. Now, there were occasions when I'd have to tap them on their legs for being disobedient about something, but never had to bring out the switch as my father had done to me so many times. My wife and I talked to them whenever they were unruly and that seemed to always solve the problem. We gave them lots of praise and hugs and kisses and told them how much we loved them.

We taught our children to be grateful for the little things in life as well as the big. To be compassionate and think about the welfare of others. As a result, they grew into law abiding adults who still not only care about their family, but their community as well.

It's a new day now. We are in the mist of many broken homes; single parent homes. It is unfortunate that one parent has to take on the role of both father and mother. Despite this situation, that parent has to still parent; that is, train and guide their children. It is that parent's responsibility to adhere to God's teachings and be that intended role model.

When it comes down to it, we must readily admit that there is no ideal household—one parent or both parents. Children are not born to automatically do the right thing. Remember we are all born as sinners. This means, we have to be taught. We have to be taught how to be affectionate. We have to be taught how to care about others. We have to be taught how to respect and be kind and generous. We have to be taught how to love. We have to be taught right from wrong.

Parenting is hard. And anyone who says otherwise is fooling himself. It is difficult and cannot be taken for granted.

But, you know, sometimes we make it more difficult than it has to be. This of course happens because we do not follow God's teachings. So many times, we think we know more than God; we have a better way of doing things. When this happens, we and the child find ourselves on the wrong end of the stick.

Genesis 18:19 says "For I know him, that he will command his children and his household after him, and they shall keep the way of the Lord…".

This scripture and so many more, say that we are to train to teach to guide our children. We are not to "spare the rod". Remember—free will; choices. When not taught/guided, children can make the wrong choices and ultimately suffer undue consequences; consequences that could have been avoided had the parent stepped in and performed his duty.

It matters not which "rod" is used. A spanking, now and then might be the answer; time-out; taking away TV or video game time; showing the child; explaining a situation. Whatever works for you, do it. Children respond in different ways; so as a parent, it behooves you to determine the most effective way to discipline your child. No magic wand here; real work is required.

We definitely want to use the rod, not spare it. I don't think any of us want to be in the Sam, Beth, Junior household. But, if you "spare the rod", you will without question, end up with a Junior in some form or fashion.

FREE WILL dictates discipline.

Perhaps the following sums it all up.

A Note Written by a Child...
Mom and Dad,
Do help me to be all that I can be.
Do give me the guidance and direction I need throughout my youth.
Do prepare me for adulthood.
Do tell me NO when I cross the line.
Do show me love and affection.
Do correct me each and every time I make wrong choices.
Do tell me when I do or say something not adhering to your teachings.
Do protect me and keep me from harm.
Do give me a hug every now and then.
Do help me to be healthy, happy, and wise.
Do help me to be proud of ME.
Do help me to love ME.
Do help me to be worthy of God's love.

REFERENCES

Aldredge, Brian; Boots, Denise Paquette; Donerly, Brian; Heide, Kathleen H.; Waite, Jennifer Rebecca. "Battered Child Syndrone:An Overview of Case Law and Legislation". Criminal Law Bulletin, ol.41, 3. p.219

Bible. King James Version

"Gun Show Loophole". Retrieved from en.wikipedia.org

Johnson, Derrick (2019). "The Persistent, Painful, and Problematic Practice of Corporal Punishment in Schools". The Striking Outlaw, Southern Poverty Law Center.

Joint HRW/ACLU (2010). statement, "Corporal Punishment in Schools and Its Effects on Academic Success". Retrieved from www.hrw.org.

Levin, John. Medfis, Eric. (2009). "Mass Murder at School and Cumulative Strain; A Sequential Model. Retrieved from researchgate.net.

NCDAS (National Center for Drug Abuse Statistics). “Drug Use Among Youth: Facts & Statistics”. Retrieved from drugabusestatistics.org.

Peterson, Jillian. Densley, James (2019). What School Shooters Have in Common. Oct.8, 2019. Education Week. Retrieved from kedweek.org.

Renzoni, Camille (2020). “Drugs and Alcohol, Driving Use in High School”. The Recovery Village. Retrieved from www.the discoveryvillage.com.

APPENDIX

Words of Encouragement

The Promise of the Holy Spirit

When you have received the Lord Jesus Christ as your savior, and have been baptized and have the holy Spirit, then you are left with a comforter to guide you.

John 14:15-21 John 14:26

15 If ye love me, keep my commandments.
16 And I will pray the Father, and he shall give
you another Comforter, that he may abide with
you forever;
17 Even the Spirit of truth; whom the world
cannot receive, because it seeth him not,
neither knoweth him: but ye know him; for he
dwelleth with you,,and shall be in you.
18 I will not leave you comfortless: I will come
to you.
19 Yet a little while, and the world seeth me no
more; but ye see me: because I live, ye shall
live also.
20 At that day ye shall know that I am thy
fatherly and ye in me, and I in you.
21 He that hath my commandments, and
keepeth them, he it is that loveth me: and he
that loveth me shall be loved of my Father, and
I will love him, and will manifest myself to him.
26 But the Comforter, which is the Holy Ghost,
whom the Father will send in my name, he shall
teach you all things, and bring all things to your
remembrance, whatsoever I said unto you.

THE BEATTITUES FROM MATTHEW 5
Blessed are the poor in spirit,
For theirs is the kingdom of heaven.

Blessed are those who mourn,
For they will be comforted.

Blessed are the meek,
For they will inherit the earth.

Blessed are those who hunger an thirst for
Righteousness, for they will be filled.

Bleesed are the merciful,
For they will be shown mercy.

Blessed are the pure in heart,
For they will see God.

Blessed are the peacemakers,
For they will be called sons of God.

Blessed are those who are persecuted because
Of righteousness, for theirs is the kingdom of
heaven.

Blessed are you when people insult you,
Persecute you and falsely say all kinds of evil
Against you because of me.

About The Author

Rev. Dr. James Cotton, PhD. Is an ordained minister living in Alexandria, Virginia with his wife Margaret of 73 years and his four adult children.

He received a Bachelor's in Church Administration, a Master's in Divinity, and a PhD in Philosophy and Theology.

Rev. Cotton is devoted to his ministry and works tirelessly to help others. He believes that the purpose of human life is to prosper and live happy in a Godly way and to help others to do the same. A person never stands so tall as when he leans down to help someone in need.

Made in the USA
Middletown, DE
28 August 2020

16972427R00076